Song of Sixpence

AND MORE FAVORITE RHYMES

Illustrated by

KRISTA BRAUCKMANN-TOWNS

JANE CHAMBLESS WRIGHT

WENDY EDELSON

ANITA NELSON

LORI NELSON FIELD

DEBBIE PINKNEY

KAREN PRITCHETT

PUBLICATIONS INTERNATIONAL, LTD.

Sing a Song
of Sixpence

Sing a song of sixpence,
    A pocket full of rye;
Four-and-twenty blackbirds
    Baked in a pie!

When the pie was opened,
    The birds began to sing!
Wasn't that a dainty dish
    To set before the king?

PETER PUMPKIN-EATER

Peter, Peter, pumpkin-eater,
    Had a wife and couldn't keep her.
He put her in a pumpkin shell,
    And there he kept her very well.

Old Mother Hubbard

Old Mother Hubbard
　　Went to the cupboard
To give her poor dog a bone.

When she got there,
　　The cupboard was bare,
And so her poor dog had none.

OLD MOTHER GOOSE

Old Mother Goose,
  When she wanted to wander,
Would ride through the air
  On a very fine gander.

THERE WAS AN OLD WOMAN

There was an old woman
   Who lived in a shoe.
She had so many children,
   She didn't know what to do.
She gave them some broth
   Without any bread.
She kissed them all sweetly
   And sent them to bed.

GEORGIE PORGIE

Georgie Porgie, pudding and pie,
　　Kissed the girls and made them cry.
When the boys came out to play,
　　Georgie Porgie ran away.

OLD KING COLE

Old King Cole
  Was a merry old soul,
And a merry old soul was he;

He called for his pipe,
   And he called for his bowl,
And he called for his fiddlers three.

LITTLE BO-PEEP

Little Bo-Peep has lost her sheep,
    And can't tell where to find them.
Leave them alone,
    And they'll come home,
Wagging their tails behind them.

HUMPTY DUMPTY

Humpty Dumpty sat on a wall;
  Humpty Dumpty had a great fall!
All the king's horses
  And all the king's men
Couldn't put Humpty together again.

Jack Sprat

Jack Sprat could eat no fat.
　　His wife could eat no lean.
And so between them both, you see,
　　They licked the platter clean.